SPACE SCIENCE
JUPITER

BY BETSY RATHBURN

Are you ready to take it to the extreme? Torque books thrust you into the action-packed world of sports, vehicles, mystery, and adventure. These books may include dirt, smoke, fire, and chilling tales.
WARNING: read at your own risk.

This edition first published in 2019 by Bellwether Media, Inc.

No part of this publication may be reproduced in whole or in part without written permission of the publisher.
For information regarding permission, write to Bellwether Media, Inc., Attention: Permissions Department,
6012 Blue Circle Drive, Minnetonka, MN 55343.

Library of Congress Cataloging-in-Publication Data

Names: Rathburn, Betsy, author.
Title: Jupiter / by Betsy Rathburn.
Description: Minneapolis, MN : Bellwether Media, Inc., [2019] | Series: Torque. Space Science | Audience: Ages 7-12. | Audience: Grades 3 to 7. | Includes bibliographical references and index.
Identifiers: LCCN 2018039179 (print) | LCCN 2018040545 (ebook) | ISBN 9781681036908 (ebook) | ISBN 9781626179721 (hardcover : alk. paper)
Subjects: LCSH: Jupiter (Planet)–Juvenile literature.
Classification: LCC QB661 (ebook) | LCC QB661 .R375 2019 (print) | DDC 523.45–dc23
LC record available at https://lccn.loc.gov/2018039179

Text copyright © 2019 by Bellwether Media, Inc. TORQUE and associated logos are trademarks and/or registered trademarks of Bellwether Media, Inc. SCHOLASTIC, CHILDREN'S PRESS, and associated logos are trademarks and/or registered trademarks of Scholastic Inc., 557 Broadway, New York, NY 10012.

Editor: Kate Moening   Designer: Andrea Schneider

Printed in the United States of America, North Mankato, MN.

TABLE OF CONTENTS

Journey to Jupiter 4
What Is Jupiter? 6
How Did Jupiter Form? 14
Where Is Jupiter Found? 16
Why Do We Study Jupiter? 18
Glossary 22
To Learn More 23
Index 24

JOURNEY TO JUPITER

It is July 2016. After five years of travel, *Juno* has arrived at a beautiful planet. The spacecraft slows down as it approaches. Then, a final blast sends it into **orbit**. Welcome to Jupiter!

Juno turns to the Sun to recharge its engine. It has already traveled 1.7 billion miles (2.8 billion kilometers) from Earth. Now the spacecraft is ready to circle Jupiter for years to come!

WHAT IS JUPITER?

Jupiter is the biggest planet in the solar system. It is 272,946 miles (439,264 kilometers) around at its widest point. That is nearly 11 times larger than Earth!

This huge planet is a gas giant. Its **atmosphere** is mostly made of hydrogen and helium. These materials mix with other gases to give Jupiter its white, brown, and red stripes.

FUN FACT

HOT AND COLD

Jupiter's outer atmosphere is around -230 degrees Fahrenheit (-146 degrees Celsius). But its core reaches more than 40,000 degrees Fahrenheit (22,204 degrees Celsius)!

JUPITER VS. EARTH SIZE COMPARISON

Huge storms take place in Jupiter's atmosphere. The most famous is the Great Red Spot. This enormous storm has been raging for at least 150 years. It is slowly **shrinking**. But it is still a little wider than Earth!

There are many other storms on Jupiter, too. They may be caused by changes in the planet's **climate**.

GREAT RED SPOT

FIRST RECORDED: 1831
WIDTH: 10,159 miles (16,350 kilometers) wide
DEPTH: about 200 miles (322 kilometers) deep
STRONGEST WINDS: 425 miles (684 kilometers) per hour
TEMPERATURE: 2,400 degrees Fahrenheit (1,316 degrees Celsius)

GREAT RED SPOT

> **FUN FACT**
>
> **ALL LIT UP**
>
> Jupiter's magnetic fields cause a light show similar to Earth's auroras, or polar lights. Jupiter's lights are the brightest of any planet!

Scientists believe a huge ocean of liquid **metallic** hydrogen lies beneath Jupiter's atmosphere. This material creates powerful **magnetic fields**. They are the strongest in the solar system!

Scientists are not sure what is below Jupiter's strange ocean. Some believe there is a solid **core**. It is likely about the size of Earth!

FUN FACT

MOONS OF JUPITER

The smallest Galilean moon is Europa. Some scientists believe it contains the ingredients for life. An ocean below its surface could contain living things!

Beyond its atmosphere, Jupiter has **rings** made of dust. The main ring is 4,350 miles (7,000 kilometers) wide! But the rings are not very thick. They are usually hard to see.

The planet has at least 79 moons. Most are very small. Their orbits take them far from Jupiter. Other moons are large. The four largest are the **Galilean moons**. They stay close to the planet!

HOW DID JUPITER FORM?

Jupiter formed from the Sun's leftover materials about 4.6 billion years ago. The force of **gravity** pulled in nearby gas and dust. Then, the planet formed into a **sphere**.

Jupiter's moons and rings are very old, too. Most of the moons were likely nearby **asteroids** pulled into the planet's orbit. The rings were created when **meteorites** hit nearby moons.

FUN FACT

NEW DISCOVERIES
Scientists who study Jupiter often make new discoveries. Its rings were first observed in 1979. In 2018, 12 new moons were discovered!

ILLUSTRATION OF PLANET FORMING

WHERE IS JUPITER FOUND?

Jupiter is the fifth-closest planet to the Sun. It orbits the star from 484 million miles (779 million kilometers) away. Its distance means Jupiter circles the Sun only once every 12 years!

Jupiter is far from Earth, too. It is about 391 million miles (629 million kilometers) away. That is the length of more than 6 billion football fields!

FUN FACT

SHORT DAYS
A day on Jupiter only lasts 9 hours and 56 minutes!

HOW FAR AWAY IS JUPITER?

JUPITER TO EARTH = 391,000,000 MILES (629,000,000 KILOMETERS)

JUPITER TO SUN = 484,000,000 MILES (779,000,000 KILOMETERS)

WHY DO WE STUDY JUPITER?

Scientists believe planets like Jupiter played important roles in the early solar system. Jupiter's size helped decide the orbit of other objects such as planets and asteroids.

But there are still unanswered questions. Where did Jupiter come from? What is at its core? The answers will help scientists study other planets more closely.

CLOUDS ON JUPITER

ILLUSTRATION OF
GALILEO PROBE

Scientists use spacecraft to study Jupiter. *Juno* has been orbiting the planet since 2016. The **probe** has instruments like cameras and **magnetometers** to help scientists learn more about Jupiter.

FUN FACT

GALILEO

Juno is the second Jupiter probe. The first was *Galileo*. It was named after Galileo Galilei, a scientist famous for the first Jupiter moon discoveries. The Galilean moons are named after him!

Juno helps scientists study the gases that make up Jupiter. Scientists take pictures of the planet's surface and make maps of its magnetic fields. Each study gives clues about how faraway planets form!

GLOSSARY

asteroids–small rocky objects that orbit the Sun

atmosphere–the gases that surround Jupiter and other planets

climate–the weather conditions in an area over a long period

core–the innermost part of Jupiter

Galilean moons–the four largest moons of Jupiter; the Galilean moons are Io, Europa, Ganymede, and Callisto.

gravity–the force that pulls objects toward one another

magnetic fields–areas around an object where a magnetic pull exists

magnetometers–instruments that study magnetic forces

metallic–made of metal

meteorites–pieces of asteroids that make it through the atmosphere of a planet or moon

orbit–a complete movement around something in a fixed pattern

probe–a spacecraft designed to study faraway objects in space

rings–groupings of rocks or ice that circle a planet

shrinking–getting smaller

sphere–a ball-shaped object

TO LEARN MORE

AT THE LIBRARY

Adamson, Thomas K. *The Secrets of Jupiter.* North Mankato, Minn.: Capstone Press, 2016.

Goldstein, Margaret J. *Discover Jupiter.* Minneapolis, Minn.: Lerner Publications, 2018.

Parker, Steve. *Probes to the Planets.* Mankato, Minn.: A+ Smart Apple Media, 2016.

ON THE WEB

FACTSURFER

Factsurfer.com gives you a safe, fun way to find more information.

1. Go to www.factsurfer.com.

2. Enter "Jupiter" into the search box.

3. Click the "Surf" button and select your book cover to see a list of related web sites.

INDEX

asteroids, 14, 18
atmosphere, 6, 7, 8, 10, 12
auroras, 10, 11
cameras, 20
climate, 8
color, 6
core, 7, 10, 18
Earth, 4, 6, 7, 8, 10, 16
Galilean moons, 12, 13, 21
Galileo, 20, 21
gases, 6, 14, 21
gravity, 14
Great Red Spot, 8, 9
Juno, 4, 5, 20, 21
magnetic fields, 10, 21

magnetometers, 20
meteorites, 14
moons, 12, 13, 14, 15, 21
ocean, 10, 12
orbit, 4, 12, 14, 16, 18
probe, 20, 21
rings, 12, 14, 15
scientists, 10, 12, 15, 18, 20, 21
size, 6, 7, 18
solar system, 6, 10, 18
sphere, 14
star, 16
storms, 8
Sun, 4, 14, 16
surface, 12, 21

The images in this book are reproduced through the courtesy of: Nerthuz, front cover, pp. 10-11 (satellite); NASA/JPL-Caltech/SwRI/MSSS/Gerald Eichstadt/Sean Doran/ NASA Images, pp. 2, 18-19; NASA, pp. 4-5 (Jupiter), 6-7; NASA/ Wikipedia, pp. 4-5 (Juno), 20; NASA/ NASA Images, p. 7 (Earth); Tristan3D, pp. 8-9; Stocktrek Images, Inc./ Alamy, p. 11 (Jupiter): mr.Timmi, p. 13 (Europa, Ganymede, Io); NASA/JPL/ DLR, NASA Images, p. 13 (Callisto); Vadim Sadovski, pp. 14-15, 21; Markus Gann, p. 16-17 (Sun); NASA/ JPL/Space Science Institute/ Wikipedia, p. 17.

523.45 R   FLT
Rathburn, Betsy,
Jupiter /

04/19